REPRESENTATION
OF THE UNIFORMS
OF THE
IMPERIAL ARMY
OF ALL RUSSIA
1790–98

REPRESENTATION OF THE UNIFORMS OF THE IMPERIAL ARMY OF ALL RUSSIA 1790–98

RAY WESTLAKE

The Naval & Military Press

© Ray Westlake. 2023

Published by

The Naval & Military Press Ltd
Unit 5 Riverside
Bellbrook Industrial Estate
Uckfield, East Sussex
TN22 1QQ
England

Tel: +44 (0) 1825 749494

www.naval-military-press.com

Acknowledgments

This book would not have been possible without the generosity of the SPL Rare Book Collection who provided the high resolution images used in this production. Also to my publisher, the Naval & Military Press, for their continued confidence in these records of military art. And as ever, my wife Claire.

This book is dedicated to John Hughes, a reliable friend of some ten, important, years.

REPRESENTATION OF THE UNIFORMS OF THE IMPERIAL ARMY OF ALL RUSSIA 1790-98
REPRESENTATION DES UNIFORMS DE L'ARMEE IMPERIALE DE TOUTES LES RUSSIES

Christian Gottfried Heinrich Geissler, draughtsman and etcher, produced this fine and important series of Russian military costumes when he spent the years 1790 to 1798 serving as the expedition artist with the Prussian zoologist and botanist Peter Simon Pallas, on his travels in the Caucasus and southern Russia. On his return to his birth town of Leipzig, Geissler published the Pallas works as well as his own illustrated accounts of Russian customs and costumes. Russian types were a favourite of foreign artists who visited or resided in Moscow or St. Petersburg.

The plates are accurately reproduced in facsimile from the deluxe version, of the larger format, of this fine series of Russian military costumes, that benefited from being both beautifully hand-coloured and heightened with gold.

Lively commentary from expert Ray Westlake on each plate enhances their usefulness for the modern uniformologist.

Seventy military figures are shown and form part of our developing range of books dedicated to uniformology, drawing on seminal works from the 18th and 19th century. They are masterpieces of military art, and important historical reference works.

The history of the Russian army in this era was linked to the name of Alexander Suvorov, a Russian general, reckoned one of a few great generals in history who never lost a battle. He fought the Turks during the Russo-Turkish War of 1787-1792 and won many victories. Suvorov's leadership also played a key role in Russian victory over the Poles during the Kosciuszko Uprising.

After Catherine II died in 1796, her son Paul succeeded her. His independent conduct of the foreign affairs of Russia plunged the country first into the Second Coalition against France in 1798, and then into armed neutrality against Britain. The new emperor drilled the Russian army on the Prussian model, which resulted in conflict with Suvorov and his subsequent removal and self-imposed exile. However, he was recalled to the army in 1798-1799.

INDEX TO PLATES

REPRESENTATION OF THE UNIFORMS OF THE IMPERIAL ARMY OF ALL RUSSIA 1790-98

Title page.

1. Un Mousquetaire des gardes d'Esmailovski

2. Brigadier de l'Infanterie.

3. Colonel des regimens Carabiniers.

4. Major General de la Cavalerie.

5. Lieutenant General de l'Artillerie.

6. Amiral de la Flotte.

7. Marechal General de l'Infanterie.

8. Un Grenadier d'Infanterie.

9. Un Soldat du Gouvernement de St. Petersbourg.

10. Un Soldat de la banque de St. Petersbourg.

11. Un Soldat du Senat.

12. Un Postillion de la Poste de St. Petersbourg.

13. Un Cosaque du Don.

14. Un Baschquire.

15. Officier du Corps Imperial des Cadet de tenue.

16. Lieutenant Colonel, Premier et second Major de l'Infanterie.

17. Un Soldat du College étranger.

18. Officier du Genie, des Mineurs et des Pioniers.

19. Officier des Bombardiers, des Canonier et des Fusiliers de l'Artillerie Major.

20. Officier du régiment de Cuirassiers de Casair

21. Officier des regiment Carabinier.

22. Officier des regimens de Dragons.

23. Officier des Housards réunis au régiment de Dragons de Pleskow.

24. Officier des troupes legered.

25. Officier de Chasseurs a Cheval.

26. Officier du régiment des Grenadiers du Corps.

27. Officier des régimens de Marine et d'Infanterie.

28. Officier des bataillons de Chasseurs a pied.

29. Officier du premier bataillon de la flotte.

30. Officier de l'Artillerie marine.

31. Officier de vaisseaux de la flotte.

32. Officier des Bombardiers de la flotille a ramer.

33. Officier de la banque de St. Petersbourg.

34. Officier de Gouvernement a St. Petersbourg.

35. Officier du College étranger.

36. Officier du Senat et de l'état des vivres.

37. Officier de la Garrison.

38. Officier des batallons de la flotte.

39. Officier des Cassaques du Don.

40. Un Chevalier Garde.

41. Un Cuirassier du Corps.

42. Un Houzard du Corps.

43. Un Cavalier des gardes a cheval.

44. Un Grenadier des garde de Preobragenski.

45. Officier du regiment des Cuirassiers du Corps.

46. Officier du régiment de Cuirassiers de l'Order militaire de St. Martyreret vainqueur George.

47. Officier du regimens de Cuirassiers de son altesse l'houtier
48. Officier de la Garde a Cheval.
49. Officier des Housards du Corps.
50. Officier des Cossaques du Corps.
51. Officier de quartier, de division et de Colonne.
52. Officier du regiment de Cuirassiers de Novotroitzk.
53. Un Bombadier de l'Artillerie de Marine.
54. Un Grenadier du premier regiment de Marine.
55. Un Mousquetaire d'un régiment de Marine et d'Infanterie.
56. Un Matelot.
57. Un Soldat de l'Etat de le vivzel.
58. Un Soldat de Garrison.
59. Un Grenadier du Corps.
60. Un Chasseur a Cheval.
61. Officier du Corps des Cadets Grecs.
62. Officier du Corps des cadets d'Artillerie et de Genie.
63. Officier du Corps de marine.
64. Officier de la Garde du Corps de Preobragenski des Compagnies de Grenadiers.
65. Officier de la Garde du Corps de Semenoyski Compagnies de Mousquetaires.
66. Un Grenadier du premier bataillon de la flotte.
67. Un Mousquetaire des bataillons de la flotte.
68. Un Chasseur d'Infanterie.
69. Un Mousquetaire d'Infanterie.
70. Un Cuirassier regiment de Casan.
71. Un Cavalier de chevaux legere.

PLATE 1

The artist shows his Russian high ranking officer of infantry posing with one hand on his hip and the other holding a baton—or is it a closed telescope? His black headdress is covered in white feathers, its brim having a deep line of gold lace. A blue coat is worn with tails reaching down several inches below the tops of high black, knee-length-boots. His rank warrants much gold lace. See how it runs in several lines all the way down the front of the coat from the collar to the skirts and forms a circle around the upper arms before falling down the back to reach the cuffs. There is more at the back of the coat arranged in single and treble lines. The waistcoat's, high collar and cuffs are red, and again richly decorated with gold. And there is a wide sash which appears black with, of course, more gold lace. Finally, a broad light blue sash is worn from the right shoulder and across the body to the left hip where it terminates in a wide bow. From their lines of canvas tents set up on hillside slopes, and after hours of preparation, battalion after battalion have marched down to parade before their commander. And here we see some of them. Blue-coated and red waistcoated, their Standards flying proud in the breeze. Their officer, accompanied by a drummer, looks across at the ranks to make sure all is as it should be on such an important inspection.

Maréchal Général de l'Infanterie

PLATE 2

See how a thick white feather has been arranged so as to travel across the headdress of this grenadier from one side to the other. Behind it sits another which this time is black. With a wide brim at the front, and what looks like a band of red, white and green at the rear, the cap is black, and with a triangular metal plate inscribed with a crown and cypher at the front. As wide lapels, deep cuffs, a lining to the turned back short jacket, and breeches, red and green dominate this detailed painting. The latter netherwear disappearing into black boots with cut out 'Vs' at the top, having two lines of shaped white lines down the outside. Brass for the buttons, which line the lapels, and have been arranged two on each cuff, with two just above those on the green of the coat. White for the belts, one being worn over the left shoulder and holding a black pouch at the back. The other at the waist and with an oval brass buckle. The grenadier stands with his bayonet fixed, the butt of his musket resting at his feet. He has come out from a tented camp set up on open ground below a range of hills to pose while one man rests on a wooden stool, two others chat, and another takes his turn at guard duty.

Un Grenadier d'Infanterie.

PLATE 3

For this painting the artist has composed a spectacular background of hills, a river with a small island upon which a cluster of trees can be seen growing, and a headland which juts out into the water. More trees on either side of the image, joined by some healthy-looking green bushes, and a small stone bridge below which flows the beginning of a steep waterfall through several boulders. On level grass stands a Lieutenant-Colonel, *'Premier et second, Major del' Infanterie.'* He wears a blue, tailed, coat with wide red lapels, each with seven gilt buttons. Open at the front, it reveals a red waistcoat edged and decorated with a gold lace. The garment providing a comfortable resting place for the officer's left hand. The plain, un-buttoned or laced, cuffs are also red. As is the coat linings which are clearly seen at the tails. There is a fine waistbelt of gold which has two black lines and holds a sword at the left hip. On the left shoulder, a fringed epaulette according to rank. White breeches are worn with high black, spurred, boots. For the headdress, a black bi-corn hat which has gold ornaments at each end, and a single gilt button at the base of a short feather tuft.

Lieutenant Colonel, Premier et second Major de l'Infanterie.

PLATE 4

In this painting artist Geissler features an officer of 'the Fleet' out for a stroll along a river bank. He is shown bright-eyed and, if his shadow is anything to go by, is walking into the sun. The artist has been generous with his detailed background. The eye is drawn across the river towards an official-looking building. Single-storied and with a grey roof, its main feature is a rotunda-type structure rising up from a columned entrance area. At the top stands a tall statue of a man holding a spear. To the left and right of the main building there are two more. Symmetrical, these are red-roofed and with columned entrance areas. A tall man, the officer walks with the aid of a long stick. His dark tailed coat falls well below his knees to where a white lining is revealed at the turnbacks. There are wide red lapels, each with six gilt buttons, and red again forming an edging for the cuffs. A white waistcoat is worn, over which can be seen a wide sash of black and gold which terminates at the left side with long tassels. Around the neck is worn a gorget which is supported by a ribbon tied at the back. Much larger than average, it appears to be charged with the Russian Imperial Eagle. For the headdress, an edging of gold lace.

Officier du premier bataillon de la flotte

PLATE 5

Another fine and detailed background from artist Geissler. Clearly St Petersburg, where he stayed on an extended visit between 1790 and 1798, the painting shows a two-storied building with shuttered windows to the left, which casts a broad shadow across a cobbled courtyard. The entrance to the place, the bank presumably, is grand. Appearing to be across a river bridge and having domed structures which support thick suspension chains. Through them has ridden a blue-coated figure wearing a black bicorn hat, a white shoulder belt and white breeches. Just to the left, and possible on his way out from the bank, a civilian carrying a large backpack can be seen against iron railings that have been cast with an arrangement of elongated ovals. Geissler's main figure is captioned as an Officer of the Bank of St Petersburg. Holding a wooden walking stick in his left gloved hand, he poses for the artist. Long, the tails of his blue coat fall down to several inches below the knees. They are adorned with gold lace, and just a hint of a white lining is visible. There are wide, yellow, lapels with large buttons, cuffs of the same colour, and a white waistcoat worn with a white cravat. A sword is carried which hangs from and elaborate belt of gold and black.

Officier de la banque de St: Petersbourg.

PLATE 6

A three-masted ship flying long red-and-white pennants lies anchored just out from the harbour entrance. All sails have been furled and there is a small rowing boat on the port side crewed by three or four men. On the starboard side another craft has left the harbour and is making its way towards the ship. The harbour walls are thick and steep. On land there is a long hut with seven windows and a red-tiled roof, and what looks like a tall ship's mast. Featured for the second time in this series is an officer of the 'Fleet Battalions.' With both arms resting on his long stick, he poses while wearing a large metal gorget suspended from a ribbon tied around his neck. The Russian Imperial insignia of a double-headed eagle is clearly shown by the artist. Wide red lapels with gilt buttons spread out across the chest to reveal a white waistcoat. There are more buttons below, and several making their way along the pocket flaps to the rear of the coat. The turnbacks on the long tails show a white lining. Gold lace and adornments for the black hat. Stout black leather for the high boots which cover the knees.

Officier des bataillons de la flotte.

PLATE 7

The artist this time has repeated the artwork used for Plate 2. Identical save for the headdress which now has a black feather instead of white draped across the top of the cap and no visible plate. This identifying the wearer on this occasion as a musketeer rather than a grenadier.

Un Mousquetaire d'un regiment de Marine et d'Infanterie.

PLATE 8

This time economical with his background, the artist in this painting features a soldier wearing a dark blue coatee which has wide red lapels, plain red cuffs and brass or gilt buttons. Red also for the breeches which have white, shaped, lace down either side. There is a single white cloth epaulette on the left shoulder, under which passes a broad buff belt. The waistbelt has an oval buckle. For the black headdress, a wide white plume which passes across the head from one side to the other, a pointed yellow metal plate and a small black feather jutting out from the left side.

Un Soldat de l'Etat de Zurzel.

PLATE 9

Shown posing against a barren landscape, this musketeer wears two medals on the left breast of his dark coat. Just buttoned in part, the garment opens up sufficiently to reveal a bright red waistcoat over which has been placed a white, brass buckled, belt. Red also for the cuffs and coat linings. The latter quite clearly seen on the long coat tails and at the left side as it turns back just below the medals. White breeches are being worn, together with white knee-length gaiters and black shoes. Notice the wig, and how the wide bicorn hat slopes to one side.

Un Mousquetaire des gardes d'Ismailovski

PLATE 10

Here we have a fine portrait of an infantry brigadier posing on a grassy mound before several ranks of his troops. All are shown wearing blue coats with red lapels and white netherwear. From the smoke in the centre of the image, it seems that a volley has just been fired by part of the line. To the left and right all are standing firm and with their arms at the 'shoulder'. Three officers are present, two standing before their companies, a third mounted. Perhaps the sound of the volley would have alerted the residents of the small village in the distance. Certainly there seems to be a look of surprise in the face of the brigadier. But unshaken he remains standing, sword drawn and with his right foot slightly forward. His coat has a red collar and cuffs, both edged with gold lace, and more of the same running all the way down to the bottom of the tails, and around the pocket flaps. Red with gold lace for the waistcoat.

Brigadier de l'Infanterie.

PLATE 11

Once again the artist has used a background view included in a previous painting—that shown in Plate 3—a spectacular background of hills, a river with a small island upon which a cluster of trees can be seen growing, and a headland which juts out into the water. More trees on either side of the image, joined by some healthy-looking green bushes, and a small stone bridge below which flows the beginning of a steep waterfall through several boulders. This time, however, he features a colonel of a carabineer regiment who takes up exactly the same pose as his fellow officer in Plate 3. The only noticeable difference in the uniform this time being that the coat is shown as a much darker blue. But here again are the red lapels, cuffs and coat linings, and the single epaulette on the left shoulder.

Colonel des régimens Carabiniers.

PLATE 12

Here we have a major-general of cavalry. He is shown posing before several large tents, one of which flies a white flag charged with a blue saltire cross. With his bayonet fixed, a blue-coated sentry can be seen just behind the general's left coat tail. The uniform, as expected, contains much gold lace and braid which can be seen as an edging to the red collar, along the top of the cuffs, down the front of the coat and on its pocket flaps. There is also vast amounts on the red waistcoat. He wears a star-shaped order on his left breast, and over his right shoulder, a crimson sash.

Major Général de la Cavalerie

PLATE 13

For this painting the artist has set a vast tented camp before a range of hills, together with a single, sloping, tree on the side of a hill to the right, several building and a cluster of more trees below a hill that seems to lead up to yet more buildings. Back at the camp, a group of soldiers dressed in red have gathered together close to a number of muskets leaning against wooden rests and what appears to be a pair of encased Standards. The picture features a lieutenant-general of artillery. He poses on a grassy mound, one arm on his right hip, his head turned to his left. His long red coat has a black collar and cuffs, its lace running thick in double lines all the way down to the tails, in two lines on the cuffs, and in several decorating the pocket flaps. The white waistcoat is also rich in gold. For the black bicorn hat, more gold lace and an ample quantity of white fur.

Lieutenant Général de l'Artillerie

PLATE 14

This busy-looking harbour, with its strong stone walls, provides a fitting setting for the featured subject of this painting. An Admiral of the Fleet no less. His white coat and blue waistcoat are absolutely smothered with decorative lace and braid. High is his blue collar, deep his cuffs. Much is to be noticed in the artist's detailed background. One man is shown looking out to sea as he stands guard by a domed-topped sentry box. Towards him, having just past a lone tree, comes a civilian. The buildings are plentiful, some with red-tiled roofs, others with many windows which suggest a barracks. The masts and top rigging of two ships can be seen, both flying long red pennants. Somewhere behind all this is a church, its tall steeple just visible on the right of the image.

Amiral de la flotte.

PLATE 15

Here we have what the artist's caption describes as, 'Un Soldat du Gouvernement de St Petersbourg.' Christian Gottfried Heinrich Geissler has been economic with his background and choses to illustrate his subject standing on a simple cobbled pavement or roadway. The uniform is plain too. A short blue coat with black lapels and cuffs, a single white cloth epaulette on the left shoulder and white pantaloons which have a black, shaped, line down the sides. White for the belts, brass or gilt for the buttons.

Un Soldat du Gouvernement de St. Petersbourg.

PLATE 16

This, '*Un Soldat de la banque de St Petersbourg*' poses with sword drawn, arm on hip, and looking off to his left. Green and yellow are the featured colours of the uniform: the former for the short jacket, which has wide turnbacks at the front to reveal more green as a lining. A plain cloth shoulder strap can be seen which is edged with yellow. The netherwear is also green. For the latter colour, yellow brightens up the jacket with its lapels, split cuffs, skirt and shoulder strap edgings. Note how the top of the jacket has been shown open so as to reveal a white cravat. A high, protruding, peak for the headdress which sits square on the wearer's head. The colours green and yellow once again featuring. The artist has been sparingly with his background, this time treating the viewer to just a simple country landscape—hills in the far distance, with a small clump of trees to the left.

Un Soldat de la banque de St. Petersbourg

PLATE 17

Un Soldat du Sénat. A colourful and bright image. The coat is blue and has wide red lapels that run down each side as far as the waist. The plain cuffs are also red, and as the eye moves down the long tailed coat, there is just a glimpse of a red lining, A single yellow epaulette is worn on the left shoulder only, under which runs a wide belt to hold a pouch behind at the hip. Yellow again, this time for the brass-buttoned waistcoat and pantaloons. White hosiery protruding just above the knee-length black boots.

Un Soldat du Sénat.

PLATE 18

Here we have an official of the St Petersburg Post Office. In his un-gloved left hand he holds a single envelope which has been sealed with red wax on the flap. Squinting slightly, he glances downwards towards the face of the communication seeking an address. The letter has come from a large black pouch carried at the front of his body, its flap sporting a circular brass plate which has been inscribed with the Russian Imperial Eagle device—the same insignia which can be seen on a triangular-shaped plate worn on the high and curved cap front. A greenish-blue tailed coat is worn which has what appears to be black cuffs. Just visible from below the correspondence-filled pouch is a waistcoat which could be buff or white.

Un Postillon de la Poste de St. Petersbourg

PLATE 19

Appearing as though it was almost floating on water like a cargo-laden ship, a long shed-like building has been included by the artist at the extreme left of his painting. His hand-written caption to the work informs that we are looking at men from the Don Cossacks, the areas of the middle and lower River Don being where the men of this regiment had originated. Across the river we now have a setting of trees, bushes and a large grassy rock. On the latter, and well-armed with his long spear, sword and a pistol tucked into his belt behind, one Cossack rests for a while seemingly deep in thought. Standing to his left, the second Cossack tightly grips his two visible weapons: his sword in the left hand, a lethal whip in the right. Roomy, and almost all blue, the coat has narrow lines of white piping on the collar, cuffs and down the front. Cross belts are worn, another much, much more narrower can just be made out. The waist belt looks brown of crimson.

Un Cosaque du Don.

PLATE 20

'Un Baschquire'. Going by his bow and quiver of arrows, the subject of this painting seems to be an archer. Peaceful he looks here, but no doubt an adversary to be respected at all times. His dress gives the impression that he would be comfortable in cold climates. Note the heavily furred headdress and collar.

Un Baschquire

PLATE 21

The artist's background for this painting shows a tented camp before a line of trees. An orderly range, all in full leaf, which range across the entire width of the image. The tents themselves are large, neat and packed closely together. To the left, two men in yellow coats stand in conversation by what could be a temporary, canvas, sentry box. Or is it fact a latrine? A luxury indeed which would complement the pointed structure close by—a form of washing facility possibly. Drawing the eye across to the right we see that two sentries have been placed as a guard over a pair of Standards which are at rest vertically against a table. This is a camp set up by a Cadet formation, the featured figure being one of its officers. Note how thick the artist has placed the lace: on the collar, cuffs, as an edging to both the long blue coat and yellow waistcoat, as decoration for a black sash which falls with heavy tassels to the left hip, and in wide lines on the hat. Also note the large gorget with its Russian Imperial Eagle device.

Officier du Corps Impérial des Cadett. de terre.

PLATE 22

In his yellow uniform, this could possibly be one of the cadets from the previous Plate 21. The artist has provided just a hint of a yellow epaulette on the left shoulder and shows a dark green colour for the lapels, cuffs and waistcoat. The cadet carries a short sword and wears a white shoulder belt.

Un Soldat du Collège étranger.

PLATE 23

Here we have an officer of Pioneers who wears a long red coat with dark lapels, cuffs and linings. A neat yellow waistcoat matches the colour of the netherwear which disappears into high, knee-length, black boots. In this painting the artist has treated us to an interesting landscape background which does much to illustrate the work of the Pioneer. Note the inclusion of the deep defensive ditch before which has been set up a field gun of brass and heavy wood. Could the enemy be billeted in those distant buildings set among trees and green bushes? Or even more likely in what appears beyond to be a fortress with high embattled walls. Beit towards houses or fortress, the way forward will be across open green fields, and that inviting winding lane. Not for the field gun, but that pile of siege mortar bombs awaiting their gunners by the bush on the right, will certainly do much to aid progress in the fight to come.

Officier du Génie, des Mineurs et des Pioniers.

PLATE 24

There again are the red-roofed houses, the inviting winding lane, green fields and ready for action field gun. The Pioneer-dug long ditch is their too. As is the neat pile of siege mortar bombs for the moment at peace among the foliage of a small bush. Yes, Christian Gottfried Heinrich Geissler has used the same background for this painting—an officer of artillery bombardiers. And yes, the uniform is the same, save that is for the single epaulette, which is now a straight line of gold braid ending with a button, and the buttons which are now gilt instead of silver. But where is the fortress? Shrouded in smoke possible, the siege having been underway for a while.

Officier des Bombardiers, des Canoniers et des Fusiliers de l'Artillerie Major.

PLATE 25

Posing on high ground above a town or village and a vast tented camp, is an of from a cuirassier regiment. His headdress, as wide as the wearer, is black and sports a white feather plume. But how striking is the short jacket and pantaloons. A bright yellow which sets a wonderful foundation for black facings, gold lace and braid. See the latter in vast quantities as an edging to the high collar, down the front of the coat and as decoration to the cuffs. Black and gold for the sash also. For the background, a winding river heads out of the town, its church steeple standing high amongst the houses, having made its way down from the distant hills looking for the sea. Could that be the officer's regiment camped down there to the left.

Officier du régiment de Cuirassiers de Cosak

PLATE 26

The artist has posed this officer beside a river, the other side of which has a collection of red-roofed houses fronted by trees and, on one side, a wooden fence. Just visible and towering high above the buildings is what appears to be the mast of a ship. On the officer's side, more trees and another fence, not in as good condition as the one previously mentioned. From a regiment of Carabiniers, he wears a long dark blue coat which has wide red lapels, red cuffs and linings. The waistcoat is also red and is covered at the waist by a black and old girdle.

Officier des regiment Carabinier.

PLATE 27

In the far distance of this painting a long range of hills runs down to a dip in the landscape where a number of tents have been set up. Across the way the artist has placed two cottages. The only building, as far as can be seen, in this wide expanse of land. By the tents, there is a single sentry who wears a short blue jacket with red pantaloons. Moving forward, we come to the feature of the image—an officer of a Dragoon regiment. Note his larger than average gorget, which bears the double-headed insignia of his country. The facing colour is red, which can be clearly seen on the lapels, cuffs and coat tail lining.

Officier des régimens de Dragons.

PLATE 28

Artist Geissler has placed his officer before a hilly landscape. Looking to the right of the painting there is a high mountain with just before it, what could be a vast city of houses and churches. It lies on the banks of a river, the other side of which can be seen a loan building. After a short expanse of flat land, the hills begin. Up they rise in stages until at the top (the far left of the image) a cottage can be seen almost swallowed up by tall trees. The subject of the picture poses with one hand on his sword, the other placed lightly on his right hip. It is here that lines of gold lace or braid have been placed each side of the bright red pantaloons. The jacket is blue, as is the pelisse which has white fur edgings.

Officier des Houssards réunis au régiment de Dragons de Pleskow.

PLATE 29

Here we have an officer of light troops who Geissler has posed in exactly the same position as the Dragoon shown in Plate 27. Both he and the landscape background are in fact identical. There are, however, differences in uniform and accoutrements. Gone for instance is the large gorget, and both the waistcoat and breeches are now white instead of yellow. The elaborate black and gold waist sash is now of a different, and more intricate, pattern. There has been a repeat of the background and here once again in the painting is the same long range of hills that run down to a dip in the landscape where a number of tents have been set up. By the tents, the same sentry with his short blue jacket and red pantaloons.

Officier des troupes légères.

PLATE 30

The artist has posed this Chasseurs à Cheval officer beside a river, the other side of which has a collection of red-roofed houses fronted by trees and, on one side, a wooden fence. Just visible and towering high above the buildings is what appears to be the mast of a ship. On the officer's side, more trees and another fence, not in as good condition as the one previously mentioned. Yes, this is the same background used by the artist in Plate 26. And yes, the featured figure is identical, save for the uniform. Note the green cords hanging from the right shoulder.

Officier de Chasseurs à Cheval

PLATE 31

Another repeated image (see Plates 27 and 29) from the artist, this time featuring an officer of Grenadiers.

Officier du régiment des Grenadiers du Corps.

PLATE 32

A larger than average gorget bearing the Russian Imperial double-headed eagle device hangs from the neck of this infantry marine officer. He wears a dark blue coat with scarlet lapels and cuffs, which is open to reveal a red waistcoat over which has been placed a fine black girdle decorated with rich gold lace. For the background, the far side of a river reveals the church spires and buildings of a busy town, the forest of ships' masts suggesting that this is some port or other.

Officier des regimens de Marine et d'Infanterie.

PLATE 33

Here we have an officer from a regiment of Chasseures a pied who is depicted drawing our attention to something on his right. He seems to be in a dull, damp, rocky place brightened only by a small placement of water. Red piping, gilt buttons and a hint of gold on the left shoulder, does much to brighten the dark uniform. Notice how the long tail of the coat terminates in a triangular shape of red piping.

Officier des bataillons de Chasseurs à pied.

PLATE 34

All is bright here in Geissler's depiction of officer of marine artillery. There's the artist's name at the bottom clearly marked on one of road cobblestones. Bright is the long-tailed jacket, bright are the breeches and hosiery. Bright too, with its white walls and clock tower, is the building in the background—a barracks possible. Dark bold lapels flow to each side of the coat to reveal a green waistcoat.

Officier de l'Artillerie marine.

PLATE 35

Here again, with its clock showing nine, its front wooden fencing sill in much need of repair, is the barracks seen in Plate 34. The figure this time is captioned as an officer of the Fleet. The same white coat, breeches and hosiery, but now the labels are distinctively green so as to match the gilt-buttoned waistcoat.

Officier de vaisseaux de la flotte.

PLATE 36

The artist has provided us with much to occupy the eye in his background to Plate 36. There across the water appears a busy town, spires and buildings tucked away behind a strong line of greenery, and just to bottom left, three figures pass by below a high brick wall. On the quayside a man wearing a red coat and black hat has found a patch of neat grass upon which he sits peacefully smoking his pipe. All around is the intricate rigging of ships. Strong and solid is the quay, the artist adding a small boat attached to it via a steel ring and a waist water outlet which can be seen discharging its cargo into the harbour. Featured is a gunnery officer who's dark blue uniform is brightened by white piping, coat linings and waistcoat.

Officier des Bombardiers de la flottille à rames.

PLATE 37

Another fine and detailed background from artist Geissler. Clearly St Petersburg, where he stayed on an extended visit between 1790 and 1798, the painting shows a two-storied building with shuttered windows to the left which casts a broad shadow across a cobbled courtyard. The entrance to the place, a Government building presumably, is grand, appearing to be across a river bridge and having domed structures which support thick suspension chains. Through them has ridden a blue-coated figure wearing a black bicorn hat, a white shoulder belt and white breeches. Just to the left, and possible on his way out from the building, a civilian carrying a large backpack can be seen against iron railings that have been cast with an arrangement of elongated ovals. Geissler's main figure is captioned as an Officer of the Government of St Petersburg. Holding a wooden walking stick in his left, gloved, hand, he poses for the artist. Long, the tails of his blue coat which fall down to several inches below the knees. There are wide, dark, lapels with large buttons, cuffs of the same colour, and a white waistcoat worn with a white cravat. A sword is carried which hangs from and elaborate belt of gold and black.

Officier de Gouvernement à St: Petersbourg.

PLATE 38

Could that be the Collage mentioned in the caption over there to the left? It seems a humble building, church-like in a way, with a plain wooden fence and what could be a well-stocked garden. The officer has made the journey down and stands posing with one hand behind his back, the other firmly gripping a long cane. Bright is the yellow uniform, its dark lapels open so as to reveal the same (black or dark green) colour. There is a high mountain peak in the far distance, forests and a little bridge over which a single figure passes.

Officier du Collège étranger.

PLATE 39

Here we have the same background used by the artist for Plate 38. The subject this time, however, is a Government official who wears a long dark blue coat with red facings, a white waistcoat and breeches with long black boots that reach well over the knee.

Officier du Sénat et de l'état des vivres.

PLATE 40

This garrison officer looks like someone not to crossed. Menacingly he glares out from the page as he stands defiant in the grounds of his domain. His coat has a red collar, cuffs and linings. His larger than overage gorget charged with the Russian Imperial double-headed Eagle. The background to the image incudes a three-storied barrack block and a rotunda building just visible above the trees. In the same blue and red, a lone sentry is no doubt looking forward to the arrival of his relief.

Officier de la Garnison.

PLATE 41

Against a mountainous background, which drops down to forest and a small stream, the Cossack officer poses for the artist. His costume green and yellow looks loose fitting and comfortable.

Officier des Cosaques du Don.

PLATE 42

Here against a plain background is a representative of the Chevalier Guarde heavy cavalry regiment. Tall black plumes burst out from the headdress like smoke from a volcano, only to be held back by a giant double-headed eagle. Just one arm and a hint of lapel is visible for the red coat as this is covered by a vastly decorated blue cuirass upon which is featured a large white star charged, again, with the Russian Imperial device. With its silver and gold lace, elaborate cross-belts, no expense has been spared in the production of this fine uniform.

Un Chevalier Garde

PLATE 43

A plain background for this cuirassier non-commissioned officer from whom the artist has captured a cheeky grin. What appears to be a plain black, domed, hat has been brought to life by a thick white plume spreading itself from one side to the other. The short, light yellow, jacket has light green lapels which on this occasion are closed. Notice how yellow cap lines fall across the back to end up hooked to one of the coat buttons. There are white cross belts and a narrow waistbelt which has a plain oval fastening. Light yellow and green also for the breeches.

Un Cuirassier du Corps.

PLATE 44

For this hussar regiment, a brown fur cap with red bag and tall plume which appears to have a representation of the Russian double-headed-eagle at its base. Green has been chosen for both the jacket and pelisse, the former having silver lace and cord, the latter a white fur lining which goes on to provide a thick edging. More generous silver lace and cord make their way down the netherwear.

Un Houzard du Corps.

PLATE 45

This senior cavalryman looks directly ahead as he poses for the artist. The tails of his blue coat fall to just above the knees where we can see that the garment's lining is red. Gauntlet gloves almost hide red cuffs. Crossing the body are two belts of red leather edged with gold. Notice how each is being worn under the shoulder straps. There is a red collar between which is a black stock and white cravat. Another red belt with gold edgings is worn at the waist, its plate oblong in shape and charged with the Russian two-headed eagle.

Un Cavalier des gardes à cheval.

PLATE 46

White feathers, black feathers and three of red all carried neatly in a bowl of leather and brass. In any other image a fair example of a still life painting, the feathers being substituted for fine and tempting fruit or blooms. Such is the headdress of this grenadier from the ancient Garde de Preobrazhensky Regiment.

Un Grenadier des gardes de Preobragenski.

PLATE 47

A vast tented camp has been set up outside a town. Having made the journey up to some high ground an officer of a cuirassier regiment poses for the artist. A bicorn hat is worn which stretches out to beyond the shoulders and much gold decorates the uniform. All is yellow, save for the deep collar which is green.

Officier du régiment des Cuirassiers du Corps

PLATE 48

Here, of course, the same background and figure. Only the colour of the collar (now black or dark blue) has changed.

Officier d. regiment de Cuirassiers de l'Ordre militaire de St. Martyr et vainqueur George.

PLATE 49

From a regiment of cuirassiers, this officer wears a white, or light buff, uniform brightened only by a collar, narrow lapels and cuffs all of red. There is also a red line which extends from the lapels to around the lower coat flaps. In the background there seems to be a tall wooden fence surrounding a village or town. Hilly is the landscape which has a stream making its way through a valley.

Officier des régimens de Cuirassiers de son Altesse l'Boucher

PLATE 50

A fine uniform for this cavalry officer. The headdress wide and heavy with gold lace, the red of the high collar barely visible below its deep gold edging. See how the dark blue coat falls down to well below the knees where its tails reveal a red lining. Following the dark blue, more gold which provides an edging that begins just behind the collar. The cuffs are red, one of them visible tucked into a rich waistcoat. The background is clearly a large barrack complex. We are looking at the parade ground possibly where a mounted officer passes by, and a wooden sentry box stands to the left.

Officier de la Garde à Cheval.

PLATE 51

Here we have a smart hussar officer wearing a green jacket ornamented by a criss-cross pattern of gold braid which journeys its way from button to button. The pelisse is also green and has a thick lining of white fur. Bright red netherwear is being worn which terminates into a pair of bright yellow boots. A red with gold decoration sabretache hangs on the left side of the officer, his curved sword just behind. With its's mountain range, small cottages, winding waterway and single-masted ship, artist Geissler has been generous with his background.

Officier des Housards du Corp.

PLATE 52

A pleasant and peaceful garden has been provided as a setting for this officer. Who, I wonder, is the statue depicting a mother and child? And for what grand event has the marque just behind been set up? The rich lawn is quiet for now.

Officier des Cosaques du Corps.

PLATE 53

Once again the artist makes use of a distant view of, possibly, St Petersburg. There are the spires and domes which reach down to the river, the trees and shrubs on the other side almost hiding what could be a signal station. Bright red lapels, waistcoat and coat linings for this officer.

Officier de quartier, de division et de Colonne.

PLATE 54

Another familiar backdrop, this time used by the author to feature an officer of a cuirassier regiment who wears yellow with light blue facings.

Officier du régiment de Cuirassiers de Novo-
twitzk.

PLATE 55

Here we have a smart bombardier from an artillery regiment. His cap sports a thick black plume that covers the headdress from side-to-side, and a brass plate. Both the short coat and netherwear appear in dark green, both the lapels and cuffs being black.

Un Bombardier de l'Artillerie de Marine.

PLATE 56

The artist provides an interesting side-on view of this grenadier. Notice the long black and white tail which hangs down from the back of the headdress and seems to have originated as a turban. And that splendid white crest which goes from one side of the helmet to the other. Moving to the coat, the short green jacket has red cuffs and two buttons on each sleeve. The same red for the netherwear. There is a white shoulder belt supporting a black pouch, upon which is a circular plate charged with the Russian Imperial Eagle.

Un Grenadier du premier régiment de Marine

PLATE 57

Plain grey coat, plain grey netherwear, plain grey hosiery, the costume of this sailor brightened only by his red sash and two tufts of red material just below the knee.

Un Matelot.

PLATE 58

The artist captions this plate as 'A garrison soldier.' The uniform is light green, the collar and cuffs red. Notice how the jacket is cut away at the front to reveal that its lining is of the same green. The flat, high-peaked cap with its white plume, matches the rest of the costume.

Un soldat de Garnison

PLATE 59

This grenadier is shown standing to attention, his black headdress and thick white feather crest doing much to add to his already natural height. Red dominates his costume as it forms the lapels, cuffs and netherwear, and a pouch belt passes below a white, fringed, epaulet. Notice how the bottom edged of the green jacket have been turned back.

Un Grenadier du Corps.

PLATE 60

Here we have a Chasseur Chaval who's dark green uniform includes black cross belts, a black sash and black boots that reach almost to the knee. A tall fur headdress is worn sporting an even taller white feather plume.

Un Chasseur à Cheval.

PLATE 61

Here we have an officer from a cadet regiment. The artist's background of a wide river presents a pleasant country scene. Across on the far side the buildings suggest a small barracks, while on the nearside a wooden fence seems to have seen better days. The officer's green jacket opens up to reveal a white waistcoat fastened with gilt buttons and a black sash decorated with three rows of thick gold lace.

Officier du Corps des Cadets Grecs.

PLATE 62

The artist's background for this painting shows a tented camp before a line of trees. An orderly range, all in full leaf, which runs across the entire width of the image. The tents themselves are large, neat and packed closely together. To the left, two men stand in conversation by what could be a temporary, canvas, sentry box. Or is it fact a latrine? A luxury indeed which would complement the pointed structure close by—a form of washing facility possibly. Drawing the eye across to the right we see that two sentries have been placed as a guard over a pair of Standards which are at rest vertically at a table. This is a camp set up by a Cadet formation, the featured figure being one of its officers. Note how thick the artist has placed the lace on the black sash which falls with heavy tassels to the left hip. Also notice the large gorget with its double-headed eagle device.

Officier du Corps des Cadets d'Artillerie et de Génie.

PLATE 63

The artist has used the same background as that in Plate 62 for this study of a Marine officer. No expense seems to have been spared on gold lace and braid for this uniform. There it is providing an edging to the lapels, on the cuffs and waistcoat. The white of the latter being only just visible. And the headdress and shoulder belt are not to be left out.

Officier du Corps de marine.

PLATE 64

Here we have an officer of the Guarde du Corps de Petersburg posing in a peaceful garden. Notice the well maintained hedges and lawn. And the two playful figures that serve as a fountain. Two elaborately decorated shoulder belts stand out, as does the large double-headed eagle gorget. The Russian emblem can be seen again on the front flap of the multi-plumed headdress.

Officier de la Garde du Corps de Préobragens- ki des Compagnies de Grenadiers.

PLATE 65

This officer of musketeers has been shown against what appears to be a harbour wall. Gold lace provides a wide edging to much of the long coat and the waistcoat. The sword belt too, with its black leather just showing through the brightness of the lines.

Officier de la Garde du Corps de Semenovski des Compagnies de Mousquetaires.

PLATE 66

The now familiar Russian double-headed eagle insignia feature this time on the cloth cap of a grenadier. The tall headdress slopes forward a little, the eagle being displayed on a yellow ground.

Un Grenadier du premier bataillon de la flotte.

PLATE 67

An interesting background to this plate which to the left shows what appears to be the remains of a tower, with something hanging out from the upper storey, standing on an island. To the right can be seen four ships, on of which is likely to be that in which the figure featured serves. He is a musketeer from one of the Fleet Battalions and is seen here walking with his musket shouldered. Red facings and brass buttons for the green jacket.

Un Mousquetaire de bataillon de la flotte

PLATE 68

The artist's sideways on view of this infantry chasseur allows us opportunity to see the equipment being carried: a large black pack, rolled cape and metal canteen. The latter is held by a think yellow cord which passes below black shoulder straps.

Un Chasseur d'Infanterie.

PLATE 69

Another sideways on view from the artist, this time featuring an infantry musketeer. Notice the piece of long black cloth which hangs down from the top of the headdress and terminates in a white tassel. Also the red lines of a turban. Held by a white belt is a large black pouch which has a circular brass plate charged with the Russian Imperial Eagle.

Un Mousquetaire d'Infanterie.

PLATE 70

Here we have a fine study of a cuirassier from the Casan Regiment. The headdress has a thick white plume that reaches from one side to the other and a pointed brass plate at the front. The jacket and netherwear decoration appear as a light yellow, while the regimental blue facing colour can be seen for the lapels, cuffs and netherwear. Notice the double yellow cord that runs from the shoulder epaulette to the front of the body where it is attached to one of the coat buttons.

Un Cuirassier du régiment de Carsan

PLATE 71

The final plate from this Christian Gottfried Heinrich Geissler collection features a cavalryman wearing a short blue jacket with red lapels closed at the front. Red also for the netherwear. Cross belts are being worn and a white cord which runs from the shoulder to the front where it is attached to one of the coat button.

Un Cavalier de chevaux legers

TITLES FOR THE MILITARY UNIFORMOLOGIST

Uniformologist: one who studies uniforms – especially military uniforms – through ages and civilisations.

We have a developing range of books dedicated to uniformology, drawing on seminal works from the 18th and 19th century. N&MP have used state-of-the-art printing technology to provide facsimile editions of these hitherto almost unattainable collections and series of military uniform plates.

The artists who illustrated these works customarily painted uniforms that were contemporary, or near contemporary, to them and had most commonly restricted their subjects to the uniforms either of their own nation or those that they had personally seen.

Some contain lively commentary from expert Ray Westlake and in some we have let the plates talk for themselves – but all, without exaggeration, are both masterpieces of military art, and important historical reference works.

REPRESENTATION OF THE CLOATHING OF HIS MAJESTY'S HOUSEHOLD 1742 – THE CLOATHING BOOK 1742

The uniforms of the whole British Army of 1742 in 94 superb colour plates. Reprint of an original and rare book commissioned by the Duke of Cumberland, victor of Culloden, and presented to King George II.

9781843428305

CAPTAIN MACDONALD'S ARTILLERY DRESS ALBUM 1625-1897

A series of watercolour sketches illustrating the dress of the Regiment.
A beautifully illustrated definitive history of the Royal Regiment of Artillery's uniforms, produced at the end of the 19th century with full colour plates.

9781783310227

www.naval-military-press.com

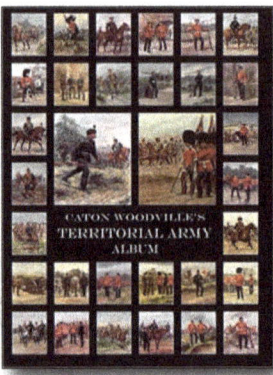

CATON WOODVILLE'S TERRITORIAL ARMY ALBUM 1908

The Naval & Military Press, in a special publication, has assembled the full colour plates painted by legendary war artist Caton Woodville depicting the Territorial Army's branches in 1908. An absolute must for anyone interested in the TA and the British Army on the eve of the Great War.

9781845747107

DERO-BECKER'S MILITARY GALLERY

A Collection of 299 Military Costume Plates of European Nations c.1815-1855 in Three Volumes

This is without doubt one of the largest suites of predominantly European military uniforms produced, and a fine reference for all military historians, wargamers and painters of European historical armies from 1800-1850.

9781474536080

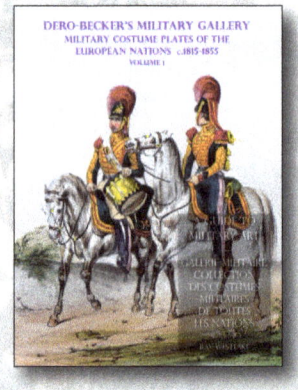

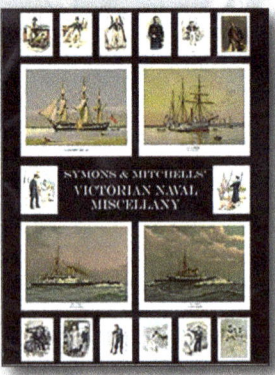

SYMONS & MITCHELLS' VICTORIAN NAVAL MISCELLANY

Sailors' Costumes and Ships of the British Fleet in Colour

A beautifully illustrated snapshot of British Navy uniforms, actions and ships produced at the later part of Queen Victoria's reign. An absolute must for anyone with an interest in the dress, and history, of the Royal Navy.

9781474536349

GILES & BUNNETT'S VICTORIAN ARMY UNIFORM ALBUM 1888

A series of fine uniform plates illustrating the dress of Her Majesty's British and Colonial Forces in her Golden Jubilee year.

A beautifully illustrated snapshot of British and Colonial Army uniforms, produced at the later part of Queen Victoria's reign. An absolute must for anyone with an interest in the dress of the army before red shifted to khaki.

9781474536356

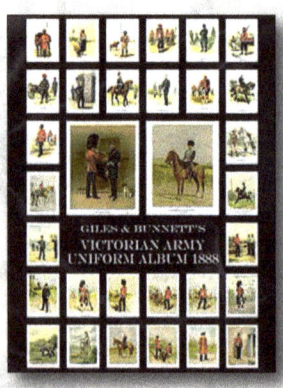

www.naval-military-press.com

BELLANGÉS'S SOLDIERS OF THE FRENCH REPUBLIC AND THE EMPIRE 1795-1814

Taken from the first German translation of 'Histoire de l'empereur Napoleon' (1840), that was enlarged for this edition with six new illustrations.

Bellangés's fifty detailed and brightly coloured uniform plates present the soldiers of the different regiments of the French Republic and the Empire in their respective costumes.

9781783318414

Richard Knötel's ARMIES OF EUROPE ILLUSTRATED (1890)

Classic descriptions complete with colour plates and vignettes by the renowned military artist and pioneer of the study of military uniform Richard Knötel, covering the armies of: The British Empire – The German Army – Austria-Hungary – Italy – France – Russia – Denmark, Sweden and Norway – Spain and Portugal – Switzerland – Holland and Belgium – Turkey and the States of the Balkan Peninsula.

9781783311750

CHARLES HAMILTON SMITH'S COSTUME OF THE ARMY OF THE BRITISH EMPIRE – ACCORDING TO THE 1814 REGULATIONS

This is a full reissuing of the 60 hand-coloured aquatint plates by I.C. Stadler, after drawings by Smith, originally produced in 1815 for the oldest commercial art gallery in the world, Colnaghi and Co. Paul Colnaghi became the official print-seller to the Prince Regent, and he was asked to organise the Royal Collection, receiving a Royal Warrant when the Prince Regent became George IV. Uniquely, many of Smith's uncoloured original drawings are also included in this edition.

9781783319916

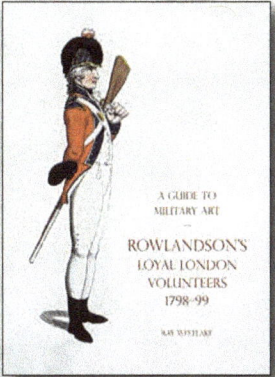

ROWLANDSON'S LOYAL LONDON VOLUNTEERS

The most original set of English military plates from the Napoleonic period – The Loyal Volunteers of London & Environs, Infantry & Cavalry, in their respective uniforms. Representing the whole of the Manual, Platoon & Funeral Exercise in 89 plates. Designed and etched by T. Rowlandson and originally published in London during 1798-99 by Ackermann. Reproduced here from high from an original volume is a full set of Rowlandson's 87 plates, together with an additional two that were to be included in some (even scarcer) bound volumes by the publisher. To accompany each plate, Ackermann prepared a page of letterpress which included details of when the corps had been formed, its uniform and names of officers. That text has been reproduced in full, together with additional notes prepared by Ray Westlake.

9781783318889

www.naval-military-press.com

MAJOR LOVETT'S MILITARY DRESS AND FIELD UNIFORMS OF THE RAJ
During the Years Leading up to the Great War

Classic representation of the British Indian Army at the height of the English Age of Empire, in 72 superb uniform plates. This is an invaluable work for anyone interested in the Indian armies and their military uniforms.

9781474536363

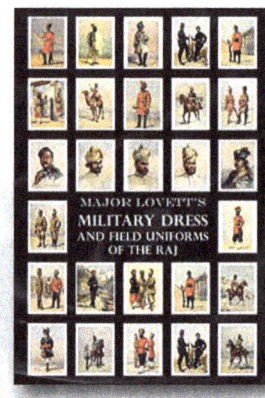

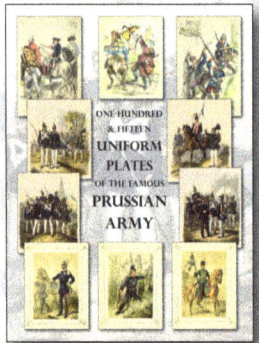

ONE HUNDRED AND FIFTEEN UNIFORM PLATES OF THE FAMOUS PRUSSIAN ARMY UNDER FREDERICK THE GREAT, FREDERICK WILLIAM IV AND PRINCE REGENT WILHELM: OMNIBUS EDITION

This is a compilation omnibus edition of three colourful 19th century military costume plate editions, detailing the Pre-Unification Prussian Army 1751-1855 in accurately hand-coloured facsimile images. Lively commentary from expert Ray Westlake on each plate enhances their historical usefulness.

9781474537551

PRUSSIAN ARMY (UNIFORM) UNDER FREDRICH WIHELM IV
PREUSSISCHE HEER, DAS, UNTER FRIEDRICH WILHELM IV

An excellent visual presentation of the Prussian Army and their uniforms under the Kaiser Friedrich Wilhelm IV. Series of 36 facsimile numbered contemporary hand-coloured lithographs. This is a colourful series of military costume plates with over 200 military figures in their 'natural surroundings': camping, in battle, on horseback, on the march, etc.

9781474537582

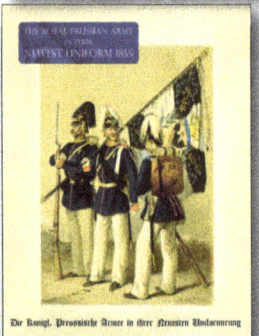

ROYAL PRUSSIAN ARMY IN THEIR NEWEST UNIFORM 1855
DIE KÖNIGL. PREUSSISCHE ARMEE IN IHRER NEUESTEN UNIFORMIRUNG

The beautiful plates depict the various uniforms of the Prussian Army as defined by the 1855 regiment. The work comprises 48 facsimile hand-coloured tinted lithographic plates of military uniforms, each mounted within a lithographed border incorporating the crowned initials of the Prussian king. A small title strip is at the bottom of each leaf, identifying the plate. Mitscher & Röstell, 1859.

9781474537582

MILITARY (UNIFORM) FROM THE TIME OF FREDERICK THE GREAT
DIE SOLDATEN FRIEDRICH'S DES GROSSEN

Thirty excellent and accurately coloured plates of the uniforms of different Prussian regiments under Frederick the Great by wood engraver Eduard Kretzschmar (1807-1858) and illustrator Adolf von Menzel (1815-1905).

9781474537575

www.naval-military-press.com

www.ingramcontent.com/pod-product-compliance
Lightning Source LLC
Chambersburg PA
CBHW061141230426
43663CB00028B/2997